MAP MY COUNTRY

MAPPING MY WORLD

CRABTREE
PUBLISHING COMPANY
WWW.CRABTREEBOOKS.COM

Published in Canada
Crabtree Publishing
616 Welland Avenue
St. Catharines, ON
L2M 5V6

Published in the United States
Crabtree Publishing
PMB 59051
350 Fifth Ave, 59th Floor
New York, NY 10118

Published in 2019 by Crabtree Publishing Company

First Published by Book Life in 2018
Copyright © 2018 Book Life

Author: Harriet Brundle

Editors: Kirsty Holmes, Janine Deschenes

Design: Matt Rumbelow

Proofreader: Kathy Middleton

Prepress technician: Tammy McGarr

Print coordinator: Katharine Berti

All facts, statistics, web addresses and URLs in this book were verified
as valid and accurate at time of writing. No responsibility for any
changes to external websites or references can be accepted by
either the author or publisher.

Photographs

All images are from Shutterstock

Printed in the U.S.A./082018/CG20180601

Library and Archives Canada Cataloguing in Publication

Brundle, Harriet, author
        Map my country / Harriet Brundle.

(Mapping my world)
Includes index.
Issued in print and electronic formats.
ISBN 978-0-7787-5002-4 (hardcover).--
ISBN 978-0-7787-5013-0 (softcover).--
ISBN 978-1-4271-2131-8 (HTML)

        1. Cartography--Juvenile literature. 2. Maps--Juvenile literature.
I. Title.

GA105.6.B785 2018   j526   C2018-902382-1
                                          C2018-902383-X

Library of Congress Cataloging-in-Publication Data

Names: Brundle, Harriet, author.
Title: Map my country / Harriet Brundle.
Description: New York : Crabtree Publishing Company, [2018] |
  Series: Mapping my world | Includes index.
Identifiers: LCCN 2018021327 (print) | LCCN 2018027506 (ebook) |
  ISBN 9781427121318 (Electronic) |
  ISBN 9780778750024 (hardcover) |
  ISBN 9780778750130 (pbk.)
Subjects: LCSH: Map reading--Juvenile literature.
Classification: LCC GA130 (ebook) | LCC GA130 .B68 2018 (print) |
  DDC 912.01/4--dc23
LC record available at https://lccn.loc.gov/2018021327

CONTENTS

Milan

Venice

FLORENCE

Pisa

ROME

Sicily

WHAT IS A MAP?

A map is a picture that gives us information about an area. It can help us learn about an area or figure out how to get to a certain location. A map can show us a lot of different things. For example, a map of a country can show roads, cities, or rivers.

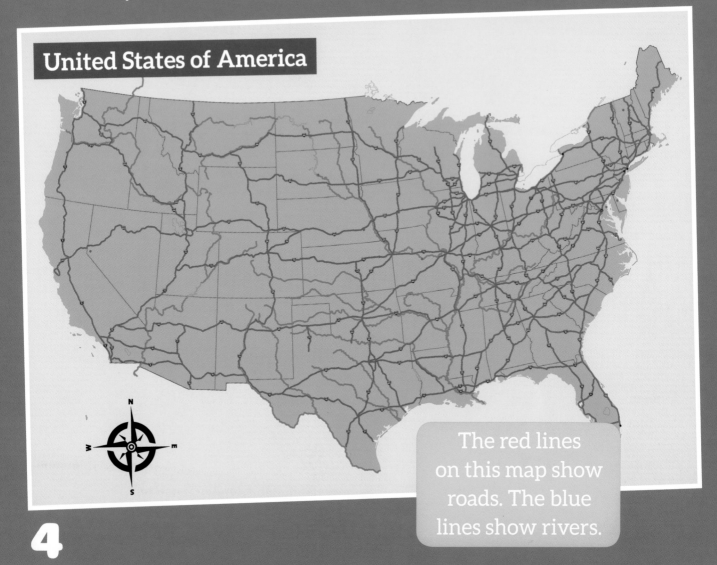

United States of America

The red lines on this map show roads. The blue lines show rivers.

Maps are drawings of real places. Some maps are printed on paper. Other maps are viewed on screens. These are called digital maps.

A map has a title. This helps the person who is reading it figure out what is on the map.

This digital map shows the countries on Earth.

Countries on Earth

GREENLAND

RUSSIA

KAZAKHSTAN

CANADA

CHINA

UNITED STATES

TURKEY

IRAN

PAKISTAN

INDIA

ALGERIA

LIBYA

EGYPT

MEXICO

CHAD

SUDAN

YEMEN

NIGERIA

ETHIOPIA

D.R. OF THE CONGO

VENEZUELA

COLOMBIA

ANGOLA

ZAMBIA

AUSTRALIA

BRAZIL

NAMIBIA

PERU

BOLIVIA

SOUTH AFRICA

ARGENTINA

USING A MAP

It is hard to see all of a large area, such as a country, from where you are standing. A map gives you something called a "bird's-eye view" of an entire area. A map shows you what a bird could see looking down from high above.

Canada

Yukon

Northwest Territories

Nunavut

British Columbia

Alberta

Saskatchewan

Manitoba

Ontario

Quebec

Newfoundland and Labrador

Prince Edward Island

Nova Scotia

New Brunswick

Compass Rose

A map usually has a **compass rose** in the corner. The points on a compass rose are marked with letters to show you which direction is north, south, east, or west. Directions help people read maps.

United States of America

Legend
- Water
- Highways
- Country border
- State border

MAP LEGEND

People use maps to learn about an area. Maps use colors and symbols, which are pictures that stand for other things, to show the locations of different things. A list of all the symbols and what they stand for usually appears in the corner of a map. This list is called a legend.

 Capital city

 City

 Road or highway

 Railway

 Mountain

 River

 Airport

Some symbols look like the things they stand for. Many maps use a triangle to stand for a mountain.

How does the legend on this map of China help you learn more about the country?

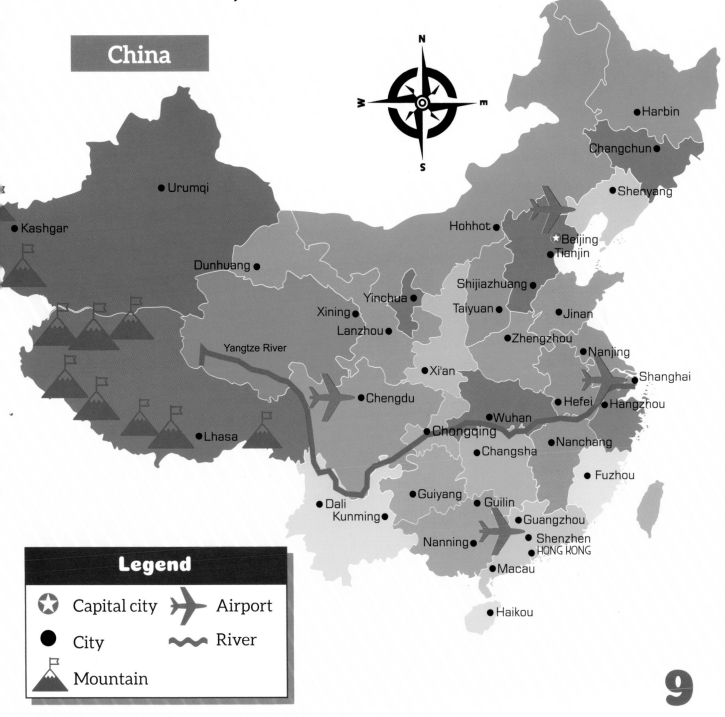

China

N
W E
S

Harbin

Changchun

Shenyang

Urumqi

Hohhot

Kashgar

Beijing
Tianjin

Dunhuang

Shijiazhuang

Jinan

Yinchua

Taiyuan

Xining

Zhengzhou

Lanzhou

Nanjing

Yangtze River

Xi'an

Shanghai

Chengdu

Hefei

Hangzhou

Wuhan

Chongqing

Nanchang

Lhasa

Changsha

Fuzhou

Guiyang

Dali
Kunming

Guilin

Guangzhou

Nanning

Shenzhen
HONG KONG

Macau

Haikou

Legend

⊗ Capital city	✈ Airport
● City	〜 River
🏔 Mountain	

SCALE

A country is too big to show on a map at its real size. Maps are shrunk, or made smaller, so they fit on paper or on a screen. All of a map's parts are shrunk by the same amount. The amount it has been shrunk is called a **scale**.

The **distance** between two points on a map stands for the real distance on the ground.

The scale shown below says that one inch on the map is about 120 miles on the ground (or 2.5 centimeters is 193 kilometers).

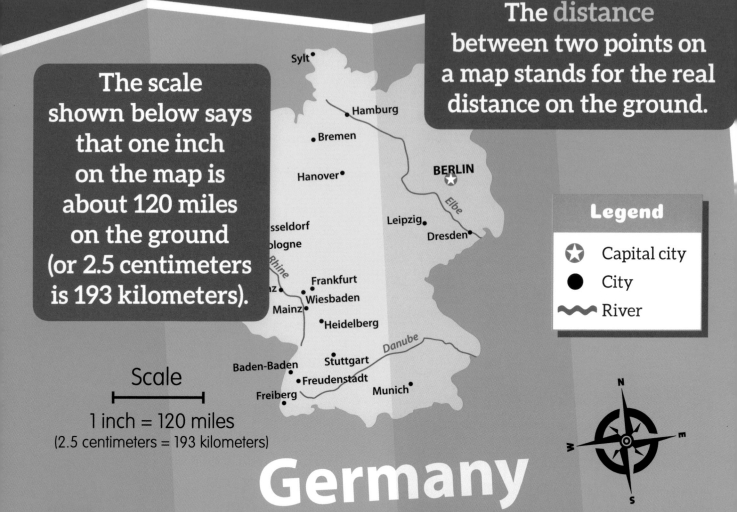

Sylt •

• Hamburg

• Bremen

Hanover•

BERLIN ☆

Elbe

sseldorf

Leipzig•

ologne

Dresden•

Rhine

• Frankfurt

az •

Wiesbaden

Mainz•

•Heidelberg

Danube

Baden-Baden • Stuttgart

• Freudenstadt

Freiberg •

Munich •

Legend

☆	Capital city
●	City
〰	River

Scale

|———————|

1 inch = 120 miles
(2.5 centimeters = 193 kilometers)

Germany

N
E
W
S

You can use the scale on a map to figure out distance on the ground. If you want to know the real distance between two cities, measure the distance on the map with a ruler. Then multiply that number by the scale.

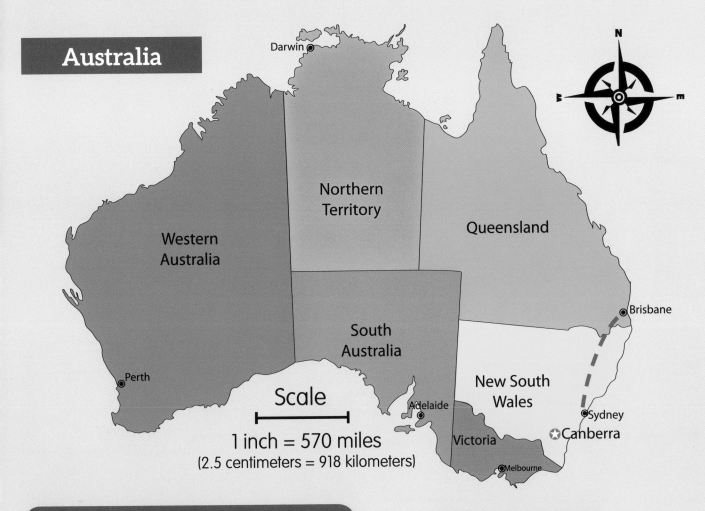

Australia

Darwin

Northern Territory

Queensland

Western Australia

Brisbane

South Australia

New South Wales

Perth

Scale

Adelaide

1 inch = 570 miles
(2.5 centimeters = 918 kilometers)

Victoria

Sydney

Canberra

Melbourne

N

Brisbane and Sydney are about one inch (2.5 cm) apart. How far apart are they on the ground?

Legend

⭐ Capital city
◉ Large city
— Border

11

DIFFERENT MAPS

There are different kinds of maps. Each kind shows different things. A **physical** map shows the shapes of the land, called landforms. Examples of landforms include rivers and mountains.

This is a **political** map. It shows how **borders** divide big areas into smaller areas. For example, countries can be divided into states, provinces, or counties.

Counties in Great Britain

Thematic maps show one special topic, such as population, or the number of people living in an area. They usually do not include the names of cities or landforms.

Population in the United States of America

Legend

Population
Largest   Smallest

This thematic map shows which states have the largest and smallest populations.

13

MAPPING A COUNTRY

There is more than one kind of country map. It can be a political map that shows how a country is divided into different parts. It can also show you which other countries are nearby.

A map of a country usually shows its capital city and other major cities.

Italy

Trentino-Alto Adige

Lombardy

Friuli-Venezia Giulia

Aosta Valley

Trento

Aosta

Venice

Trieste

Milan

Veneto

Piedmont

Turin

Genoa

Bologna

Emilia-Romagna

Liguria

Florence

Ancona

Marche

Tuscany

Perugia

Umbria

Abruzzo

L'Aquila

Molise

Rome

Campobasso

Lazio

Apulia

Bari

Naples

Potenza

Campania

Basilicata

Sardinia

Calabria

Catanzaro

Cagliari

Sicily

Palermo

Legend

⭐ Capital city

◉ Major city

— Border

Another way to map a country is to make a physical map. This shows the country's landforms and bodies of water.

A country map can also show physical and political features at the same time. This map shows landforms as well as borders.

Canada

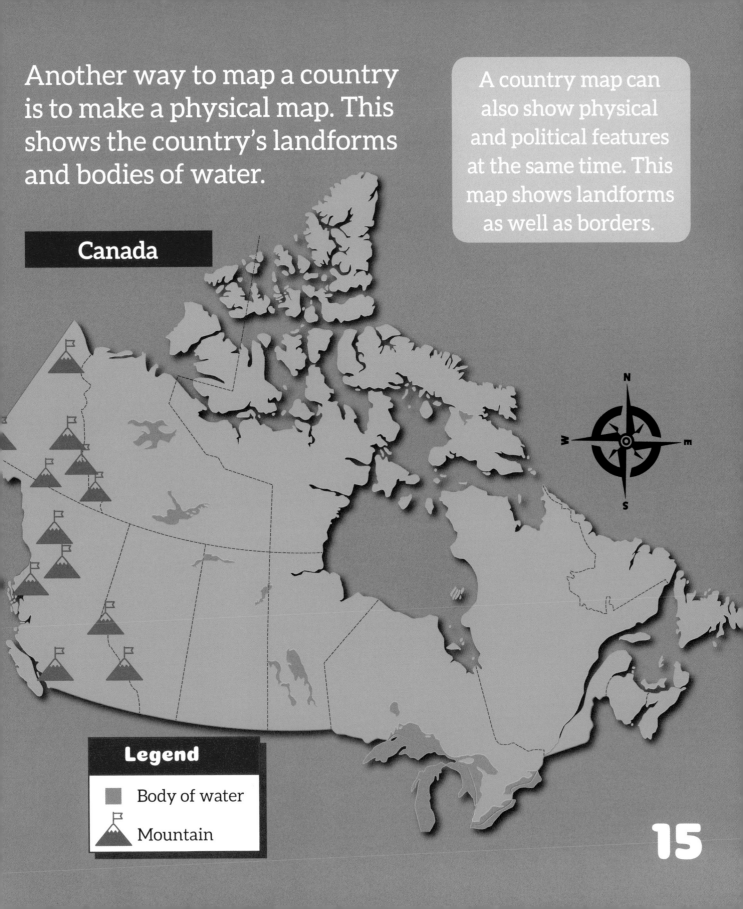

Legend

■ Body of water

⛰ Mountain

HOW DO WE USE COUNTRY MAPS?

If you wanted to travel somewhere you have never been, you can use a map of that country to see which cities you want to visit. It can tell you the cities in which important landmarks, such as ancient buildings, are found.

MILAN

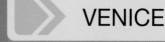

VENICE

FLORENCE

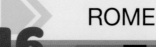

ROME

Country maps might also show how cities are linked by different roads and other types of transportation within a country. This can help you plan the transportation routes you will follow when you visit.

Railways in Russia

RUSSIA

Yaroslavl
MOSCOW
Kirov
Perm
Yekaterinburg
Tyumen
Omsk
Novosibirsk
Krasnoyarsk
Taishet
Bratsk
Ust-Kut
Lake Baikal
Severobaikalsk
Irkutsk
Ulan Ude
Chita
Naushki
Zabaikalsk
Tynda
Skovorodino
Belogorsk
Komsomolsk-on-Amur
Sovetskaya Gavan
Khabarovsk
Ussuriisk
VLADIVOSTOK

Legend
—— Trans-Siberian
—— Baikal-Amur Mainline
—— Trans-Manchurian
—— Trans-Mongolian

17

USING A GRID

Country maps sometimes include grids. Grids are horizontal and vertical lines on a map that help show the position of places and objects. Grids can help you find the location of something on a country map more easily.

World Map

ARCTIC OCEAN

GREENLAND

EUROPE

ASIA

PACIFIC OCEAN

AFRICA

NORTH AMERICA

ATLANTIC OCEAN

AUSTRALIA

PACIFIC OCEAN

SOUTH AMERICA

SOUTHERN OCEAN

ANTAR

Map grids often use letters and numbers to help locate objects on a map. Look at the map of Mexico below. The city Merida is located in the column marked with the letter J, and in the row marked with the number 6. Someone using the grid would say Merida is located at J6.

What city would you find at D4? What is the location of Mexico's capital city?

Mexico

Hermosillo

Merida

Xalapa

Mexico City

Legend
⭐ Capital city
◉ Large city

MAP ACTIUITY

Imagine you are welcoming a visitor to your country. To plan their trip, they need to learn important information about the different areas, landmarks, landforms, and transportation in your country.

It is your job to create a map to help a visitor plan their trip to your country.

MAKE A LIST

First, make a list of the information a visitor would need to know about your country. It might help to imagine you were visiting a country for the first time. What would you like to know about a new country?

Roads

Rivers

Capital city

Mountains

Tallest building

Airports

Think about how a map might show each piece of information in your list.

CREATE A LEGEND

Create symbols for each piece of information you want to include on your map. Then, make a legend of the symbols and what they stand for. Look back through the legends in this book to help you!

If you are not sure, ask an adult for ideas!

MAKING A MAP

With help from an adult, print a blank map of your country. Use your legend to add symbols to the map. Look at a real map of your country or ask an adult for help. Don't forget to add a title and a compass rose!

Use the compass rose to help give a visitor directions, such as:
"The mountains are in the west."
"The capital city is on the east coast."

GLOSSARY AND INDEX

GLOSSARY

area A specific place, such as land

bird's-eye view Looking down on something from high above

borders The boundary separating two areas, usually drawn with a line

capital city Usually, the city in which a country's government is located

compass rose   A map part that shows which ways point north, south, east, and west

digital Relating to computers

distance A space between two points

landmarks Features of a place that are easily recognized and usually have some importance

legend A map part that lists symbols and their meanings

physical Something we can notice using our body's senses, such as touch

political Relating to government

scale The amount by which everything on a map has been shrunk so it fits on a page or screen

thematic Relating to a specific theme, or subject

INDEX